WOODSON

# Breezier, Cheesier, Newest, and Bluest

## What Are Comparatives and Superlatives?

To my friends at Hainerberg Elementary School in Wiesbaden, Germany

—B.P.C.

Comparatives:
Forms of describing words that compare two things

Superlatives:
Forms of describing words that compare three or more things

# Breezier, Cheesier, Newest, and Bluest

## What Are Comparatives and Superlatives?

by Brian P. Cleary
illustrations by Brian Gable

M MILLBROOK PRESS / MINNEAPOLIS

# Comparatives

all help describe things.
Most end in e-r,

like **hotter** day
and **longer** way
and **faster, sleeker** car.

See how they compare two things,
like long when paired with longer?

6

They help distinguish by degree,
like strong
compared with stronger.

cooler, crueler,

louder, prouder,

hairier, and scarier—

these are all comparatives,
like mellower and merrier.

Try taking a
describing word,
like bright.

Now add e-r.

You've made it a comparative to name the brighter star!

But sometimes, you don't add e-r. Instead, you reach for "more,"

as in more tired,

more beautiful,

and more impressive store.

other times, comparatives,
like those I've listed here,

GOOD    BETTER

BAD    WORSE

FAR    FARTHER

seem to have no type of rule
to which they all adhere.

*Superlatives* compare as well
but speak of an extreme—

the tallest girl, the longest curl,
the highest balance beam.

17

"Tall" is a describing word, and **taller** is comparative.

Tallest is Superlative.
You following my narrative?

# Most times, a superlative will end in e-s-t:

the meanest dog,

the
greenest frog,

the fanciest TV.

It's one up from comparative,
like newest topping newer,

BEST

BETTER

GOOD

# smartest up from smarter,

# and bluest over bluer.

23

Superlatives are breeziest

and chattiest

and cheesiest,

24

funniest and sunniest

and quietest and queasiest.

SHH!

25

Most modern and most fun
are two examples I can give.

These words can be quite difficult,
but study them with zest

So that your "good" gets better and your "better" will be best!

So What are comparatives and Superlatives? Do you know?

# How to Form Comparatives and Superlatives

**Usually, add -er or -est to the end of the adjective (describing word).**

| | | |
|---|---|---|
| tall | taller | tallest |
| long | longer | longest |

**If a one-syllable adjective ends in an e, simply add -r or -st.**

| | | |
|---|---|---|
| blue | bluer | bluest |
| large | larger | largest |

**If a one-syllable adjective ends in a consonant with a vowel right before it, double the consonant before adding -er or -est.**

| | | |
|---|---|---|
| big | bigger | biggest |
| thin | thinner | thinnest |

**If an adjective ends in y, change the -y to -i and add -er or -est.**

| | | |
|---|---|---|
| happy | happier | happiest |
| lucky | luckier | luckiest |

**With many other two-syllable adjectives, use "more" or "most."**

| | | |
|---|---|---|
| pleasant | more pleasant | most pleasant |
| thoughtful | more thoughtful | most thoughtful |

**Other adjectives don't follow any pattern.**

| | | |
|---|---|---|
| far | farther | farthest |
| bad | worse | worst |
| many | more | most |

Find activities, games, and more at
www.brianpcleary.com

## ABOUT THE AUTHOR & THE ILLUSTRATOR

**BRIAN P. CLEARY** is the author of the best-selling *Words Are CATegorical*® series as well as the *Math Is CATegorical*®, *Food Is CATegorical*™, *Animal Groups Are CATegorical*™, *Adventures in Memory*™, and *Sounds Like Reading*® series. He has also written *Do You Know Dewey? Exploring the Dewey Decimal System*, *Six Sheep Sip Thick Shakes: And Other Tricky Tongue Twisters*, and several other books. Mr. Cleary lives in Cleveland, Ohio.

**BRIAN GABLE** is the illustrator of many *Words Are CATegorical*® books and the *Math Is CATegorical*® series. Mr. Gable also works as a political cartoonist for the *Globe and Mail* newspaper in Toronto, Canada.

Millbrook Press
A division of Lerner Publishing Group, Inc.
241 First Avenue North
Minneapolis, MN 55401 U.S.A.

Website address: www.lernerbooks.com

Main body text set in RandumTEMP 35/48.
Typeface provided by House Industries.

Library of Congress Cataloging-in-Publication Data

Cleary, Brian P., 1959—
    Breezier, cheesier, newest, and bluest : what are comparatives and superlatives? / by Brian P. Cleary ; illustrations by Brian Gable.
       p.   cm. — (Words are CATegorical)
    ISBN 978—0—7613—5362—1 (lib. bdg. : alk. paper)
    1. Grammar, comparative and general—Adjective—Juvenile literature. 2. Comparison (Grammar)—Juvenile literature.  I. Gable, Brian, 1949—, ill.  II. Title.
    PZ73.C54 2013
    428.1—dc23                                                                    2012019105

Manufactured in the United States of America
1 — DP — 12/31/12